Cathedral Cats

Also available from Collins by Richard Surman

Church Cats

Cathedral Cats

Richard Surman

Collins

Collins
a division of HarperCollins Publishers
77–85 Fulham Palace Road, London w6 8jb
www.collins.co.uk

First published in Great Britain in 2005 by HarperCollins Publishers.

This edition published 2006.

10 9 8 7 6 5 4 3 2 1

A catalogue record for this book is available from the British Library.

isbn–10   0-00-723563-1

isbn–13   978-0-00-723563-6

Printed and bound in Hong Kong by Printing Express

Collins

Contents

Introduction

'A man has to work so hard so that something of his personality stays alive. A tomcat has it so easy, he has only to spray and his presence is there for years on rainy days'

Albert Einstein

I'm not shy about my enduring admiration for cats. I grew up with them, and carry the scars to prove it. I regularly perform the supreme and nauseating sacrifice of opening tinned cat food at six o'clock in the morning. They share my office, every nook and cranny of our home. They dig their claws into my shins as a sign of pure pleasure, and magically become a deadweight on my lap whenever I want to move.

So what do I get in return? Good conversation, and (mostly) uncontentious company. No one will ever convince me that my own two Burmese cats don't talk to me, and it's not just about food either: the weather, politics, art; you name it, my cats have an opinion. Cats are the most fascinating, enchanting, exasperating and contrary of all nature's creatures. They do not substitute for human relationships, they complement them.

The cats portrayed in this new collection of *Cathedral Cats* cover the whole gamut, ranging from farm cats like Lichfield Cathedral's Kim, to aristocrats such as Chester Cathedral's Olsen and Hansen. But no matter what the lineage of each cat is, they all have these essential feline features in common: a flagrant disregard for rules and convention; an uncanny tendency to identify and do exactly the opposite of what is wanted; an innate belief in their right to go anywhere they want; an ability to soothe and lower one's blood pressure; and astonishing grace and dexterity. It would be fanciful and romantic to imagine that in past times cats were welcomed into cathedrals for any reason other than their skills at keeping down vermin, but today the number of cathedrals that good-humouredly tolerate the presence of cats is impressive. Maybe it has to do with the type of person that lives and works in today's cathedrals: independent, and perhaps slightly idiosyncratic – the ideal companion for such independent and idiosyncratic animals.

As for the cathedrals, they are a strange combination of the magnificent and the everyday. On one hand there are the awe-

LEFT
Steve Mellor in conversation with Wolfie
ABOVE
Leofric, featured in Country Living

inspiring architecture and settings of these great buildings, while on the other hand there are all the human elements that have brought about these monolithic expressions of faith and power. Even the grandest cathedral has its human aspect, in the lives of those who live and work in it, and in its history and construction.

Many people helped me find a new line up of cathedral cats. In particular, I'd like to thank Pauline Hawkins at Lichfield Cathedral, Catherine Spender, Simon Lole and Alun Williams at Salisbury Cathedral, Tom Morton at Portsmouth Cathedral, Angela Prior at Canterbury Cathedral, Fiona Barnaby and Nicholas Fry at Chester Cathedral, Penelope Utting at Chichester Cathedral, Alison Chambers at Hereford Cathedral, Rosemary Murgatroyd at Ripon Cathedral, Sarah Friswell at St Edmundsbury Cathedral, Anna Davidson at St Mary's Episcopal Cathedral, Jackie Pope and Joanne Green at Westminster Abbey, Fiona Price at Gloucester Cathedral, Susie Arnold at Worcester Cathedral, Chris Stone at Rochester Cathedral and Stephen Wickner at Ely Cathedral.

I'm also very grateful to Adam Munthe for providing me with a suitably eccentric and secluded hideaway in which to write, and of course to Ian Metcalfe at Collins for providing me with the opportunity to tackle anew a cherished topic, Cathedral Cats.

For my children and grandchildren

Daisy and Lazarus
St Edmundsbury

'The cat, which is a solitary beast, is single minded and goes its way alone; but the dog, like his master, is confused in his mind'
H.G. Wells

With a home that borders leafy abbey churchyard grounds, a ruined castle and a large cathedral, Daisy and Lazarus have one of the most extensive territories of all the cats in this book. And for a cat named Lazarus, what more suitable territory than a graveyard!

Catherine Todd, Rector of the Horringe Benefices, her husband Andrew, Residentiary Canon at St Edmundsbury Cathedral, and their three children, Benedict, Hannah and

THE CATHEDRAL

Unlike many of Britain's cathedrals, the final shapes of which were more or less determined in the middle ages, St Edmundsbury has acquired its present appearance since the 18th century, with the central lantern tower only recently completed.

Little of the substance of the original Benedictine Abbey of St Edmund remains, but there are some interesting remnants – the rebuilt abbey gatehouse, the excavated footings of the eastern end of the abbey, and the curious site of houses incorporated into the ruined western end of the abbey church. The present cathedral is half the length of the old abbey, which gives a pretty good idea of the scale of the original monastic buildings.

Lydia, live in a Georgian house that fronts on to the main road. Bury St Edmunds is a busy town, so the world outside the front door is a no-go zone for the cats. Fortunately for Daisy and Lazarus, the back of the house gives onto safer territory. It overlooks the delightful tree-lined promenades and crumbling gravestones of the old abbey churchyard, and enjoys a fine view of the entire length of the cathedral, complete with its magnificent new crossing tower. I was curious to know how far the cats roamed within this vast area, and Catherine thought that they went no further than the old abbey church. But I saw Lazarus nipping around the east end of the cathedral and heading for the knot garden and castle with the determination of someone who knows exactly where he's going.

The cats came from different litters of British Short-hairs. Lazarus was a weak kitten who had been abandoned, and the breeder placed him in the same litter as Daisy to see if he would revive, which he did

– and received his name in tribute to the unexpected recovery. My brief observations of both cats don't entirely align with those of the family. I was told that Daisy is more adventurous than Lazarus, but it was Lazarus that was slinking along the side of the cathedral, Lazarus who stalked off confidently in the direction of the knot

OPENING PAGE

Lazarus: a passion for brown bread

ABOVE

The graveyard is Lazarus's favourite playground

OPPOSITE

Daisy, lurking by the cathedral

garden and ruined castle; Daisy was just rolling around on an old gravestone and hiding under a neighbour's car.

The two cats live together in a state of entente demi-cordiale. They'll occupy the same room, pass relatively close to each other – and that's as far as it goes. Lazarus will insist on having the occasional tussle with Daisy; no one is sure why, as he always comes off worse. With this relationship of grudging tolerance in place, both cats generally go their separate ways.

The gardens and riverside meadows are a popular place for picnics, but the two cats have not yet worked out the tourist potential for acting as a team. Maybe neither has the need, as Daisy has found out that chapter meetings can be pretty productive, especially in other people's houses, where she can anticipate a variety of menus. For his part, Lazarus has developed some very strange food habits, principal among which is a

passion for granary bread.

Both cats have followed the construction of the new cathedral tower, from the shelter of the ruined western end of the old abbey church. The scaffolding has provided limitless opportunities for Daisy to view her kingdom while Lazarus, unimpressed by her acrobatic feats, is more interested in finding a friendly baker.

Rhubarb, Fungus and Magic
Canterbury Cathedral

'One cat just leads to another'
Ernest Hemingway

There is a cacophony of cats at Canterbury Cathedral – choir cats, school cats, canonical cats and visiting cats. Such a vigorous feline population is hardly out of character for a place that has always been a hive of activity; down the centuries Canterbury Cathedral has thrived on the visits of pilgrims to the shrine of St Thomas à Becket, and tourists come to see the tombs of Henry VI, his wife Joan of Navarre, and Edward the Black Prince.

THE CATHEDRAL

Canterbury's imposing cathedral almost overpowers the city that surrounds it, in physical terms and also in the weight of its history.

The original cathedral, built by St Augustine, was destroyed in a fire in 1067, and again fire destroyed much of its Norman replacement, although the shrine of St Thomas à Becket was spared (only to be destroyed later by Cromwell's troops). The tombs of Henry VI and his wife Joan of Navarre, and of Edward, the Black Prince survived the Reformation. Today Canterbury Cathedral remains not just a tourist destination but a place of pilgimage and a worldwide symbol for Christianity.

Adjacent to the Great Cloisters, in a house that forms part of a medieval gateway, live two cats, Rhubarb and Fungus – mother and daughter. The household in which they live is best described as an ecclesiastical ark, and is presided over by Canon Edward Condry, Canon Treasurer at the cathedral, his wife Sarah and their four children, Fran, Felix, Jerome and Hannah, who are nominally responsible for regulating the animal affairs of the household.

Fungus and Rhubarb are members of a varied household – both cats have had to make major adjustments to their natural inclinations; Fungus, when really pressed for somewhere peaceful quiet and warm to lay her head, pulls up the lid on Little Nell's cage, clambers in and snuggles up to her (Little Nell is a guinea pig). As for the dogs of the house – Jumble, Tigger and Jim – the cats will sometimes use them as scratching posts, but for the most part, they are ignored. This approach has not been entirely successful:

cats can cope with being ignored, but an ignored dog just tries harder and harder to attract attention. For an intent cat, there is nothing worse than a dog nosing in, butting the cat for attention and whacking its tail loudly against a nearby dustbin. If life gets a bit hectic they wander together over to the cloisters, where they charm the occasional edible treat from cathedral visitors.

Occasionally their timing is out, and they come nose to nose with Magic, another cathedral cat at Canterbury.

Magic also likes the cloisters. She goes there regularly and when she finds Fungus and Rhubarb there as well, the cloisters echo to distinctly unholy sounds: it's a bit like buskers competing for space. Magic lived in

OPENING PAGE

Rhubarb and Fungus, trying unsuccessfully to ignore Tigger the dog

LEFT

Magic: unmusical encounters with Fungus and Rhubarb in the cloisters

RIGHT

Rhubarb keeps a wary eye on the cloisters

Not even the dogs can follow Fungus out of the window
Magic's magical view of the cathedral

the Condry's old house before moving to another part of the cathedral precincts with her family, the Rev. Dr Canon Richard Marsh, his wife Elizabeth, and their daughter Phoebe. She loves her new house at the cathedral. At the end of a large private garden are the old city walls, on which she sits, watching the outside world scurry by. At the other end, the Bell Harry Tower rises majestically over the cathedral nave, in front of which can be seen the Corona chapel, the original home of St Thomas à Becket's relics.

Visits to the deanery are a regular item in her diary, although one day she had to explain indignantly – and ultimately unconvincingly – that she was only looking at the whole salmon laid out for lunch. And unlike Rhubarb and Fungus, Magic has found her way into the cathedral, another regular part of her perambulations around her precinct. The Good Friday services perplexed her a little: they are very long, so she distracted herself (and much of the congregation) by hopping on and off the canons' stalls, eventually settling with a sigh of resignation to an extended grooming session. She enjoys being with the choir too: this seems to be a favourite pastime for cathedral cats, and Magic has stolen the show more than once! But on a quiet summer's evening, with the cathedral almost entirely to herself, Magic likes nothing more than to stretch out on the throne of St Augustine, having a good wash while she plans the next day's itinerary.

Tomkins
Chelmsford Cathedral

'Most of us rather like our cats to have a streak of wickedness. I should not feel quite easy in the company of any cat that walked about the house with a saintly expression'

Beverley Nichols

An important part of the welcome given to visitors of the new Cathedral Centre of Chelmsford Cathedral is provided by Tomkins, a splendid, portly black and white cat named after the Elizabethan composer Thomas Tomkins, and owned by Peter Nardone, organist and Director of Music at Chelmsford Cathedral.

Tomkins is a rescue cat in every sense. When first found, he was in the garden of a derelict house in South London, frantically

THE CATHEDRAL

One of the smallest cathedrals in England, Chelmsford Cathedral serves the second largest diocese, with a population of over two and half million, covering some 600 parishes, as well as the suburban boroughs of East London.

Bishop Maurice – Lord of the Manor of Chelmsford – inspired the bridging of the river Chelmer, and as a result of the regular flow of traffic between London and Colchester, a thriving settlement sprang up, and with it the parish church of St Mary. Rebuilt in the 15th century, the church finally became a cathedral in 1914.

struggling to rid himself of a kitten collar, not because he disliked collars on principle, but because he was two years old, and the collar around his neck was for a six-month kitten: it was slowly strangling him. The fact that Tomkins had survived at all was a tribute to his strength and determination. Relieved of the collar, Tomkins was transformed into a character brimming over with gratitude and confidence, and through the efforts of the Cats Protection League, was introduced to Peter Nardone. Tomkins was Peter's first cat (and Peter probably Tomkins' first consistent human contact) and he rewarded Peter's kindness with the kind of devotion more commonly expected of dogs. When Peter moved to his current position at Chelmsford Cathedral, he and Tomkins took up residence in a secluded house on the edge of the cathedral gardens, separated from the cathedral by the recently built Cathedral Centre, and a busy road – which Tomkins has the good sense not to cross. The cathedral is a modest, but airy and pleasing, gothic

building and it is noted for its vibrant parish life and music, as well as being the venue for a renowned annual music and arts festival.

In a secluded grotto in the gardens stands a statue of St Francis of Assissi (patron saint of all animals), to which Tomkins started to pay regular visits. Some have speculated that in the cause of good public relations, Tomkins had decided that devout postures might serve as a diversion from his enthusiastic policing of other cats in the gardens. Whatever the explanation, Peter worries that over time the expression on the saint's face seems to have become slightly less benign, more exasperated, almost disapproving; but maybe it's just a trick of the light.

Around the time of the lively annual festival, Tomkins entertains and is entertained by the artists, performers, international musicians and groups who pass through here. Tomkins also diverts the many visitors from North America who come to Chelmsford; the South Porch was enhanced in the 1950s as a tribute to the endeavours and sacrifices of USAF air crews based in the area during the Second World War. George Washington's arms are also on display in the South Porch (his great-great-grandfather was a rector in Essex.) And if the choristers happen to be en route from the cathedral, he happily brings up the rear, rather like a sheep cat.

But for all his adventurings outside the home, inside it Tomkins leads a tranquil existence: every day he goes, tail lifted in greeting, to meet the postman. He always calls when the newspapers come through the letter box (though this may have more to do with his habit of sleeping on the doormat than a deliberate policy of helpfulness).

There is one area of dissonance in all this domestic harmony. While Tomkins may bear the name of a composer, it doesn't follow that he likes music, and in the early days the sound of the piano being played was enough to drive Tomkins to drink (milk laced with brandy, please). No amount of wailing or attacking the hammers inside the piano could deter Peter from playing. These days Tomkins is a little more prepared: at the sound of the grand piano being opened, he makes his way to the guest bedroom and sticks his head under a pillow.

Olsen and Hansen
Chester Cathedral

'There are two means of refuge from the miseries of life: music and cats'
Albert Schweitzer

The first sign of the cats in residence at Chester Cathedral is a small board, with 'Beware of the Cats' on it, at the entrance to the Bishop's house. Olsen and Hansen, a Siamese chocolate point and oriental red respectively, often sit at the top of the steps, keeping a watch over the adjacent cathedral and approaching visitors.

The cathedral whose environs they survey has a chequered history: with bits in it from every century since the tenth, the cathedral

THE CATHEDRAL

In the tenth century it provided a refuge for nuns from Repton rescuing the remains of St Werburgh from an invading Danish army, and in due course the existing church was rededicated to her by Aethelflaed, daughter of Alfred the Great. Having become a monastery it narrowly escaped destruction at Henry VIII's dissolution of the same and became a cathedral in 1541, but deteriorated thereafter – Daniel Defoe commented on the disintegration of the stonework, and only after extensive repair and restoration by Sir Gilbert Scott was the cathedral able to reopen for use in the early twentieth century.

OPENING PAGE
Olsen and Hansen: a mild-mannered stand-off
OPPOSITE RIGHT
An infallible nose for food
BELOW
Hansen is determined to find out where Olsen goes at night

has been significantly rebuilt three times. The first church was replaced with a Norman abbey by Hugh (Lupus), Earl of Chester, as a celestial insurance policy against a somewhat wild style of life. Then, in the thirteenth century, monks built over the Norman church, to form the basis of the present-day cathedral.

Olsen and Hansen live with the Bishop of Chester, the Rt Rev. Dr Peter Forster and his family, in a rambling Georgian building in the middle of the Cathedral Close. Olsen came to Chester with the family and his friend Murphy, a boisterous Golden Retriever. Hansen is a newcomer, and despite an initial period of deep gloom on Olsen's part at the arrival of this feline Johnny-come-lately, the two cats have reached an accord (with Murphy acting as go-between).

After introducing himself around the cathedral close and getting locked in the free-standing 1970s bell tower, Olsen was

tempted to dismiss the religious life. He turned instead to the lure of nights in the city. Olsen eventually found the ideal surroundings for his inscrutable and laid-back style: a city jazz club. According to the club owner, Pauline Thomson, Olsen just strolled in one night and wandered round talking to customers, staff and musicians, then settled down to listen to the music. He became a regular visitor and after a tenor sax player had decided that Olsen was a stray and might need a home, a bill (for food and drinks!) was attached to Olsen as a tracing device. The family responded and were assured that Olsen was always welcome, and would continue to get complimentary entrance and alimentation!

Hansen has built up his own social life within and around the Bishop's residence, languidly and vocally joining in social occasions. Being much younger, Hansen has been kept ignorant of Olsen's secret life but as he becomes more settled, he takes increasing interest in Olsen's doings, and when he can tear himself away from the warmth of the kitchen stove, can be seen pacing around the large garden, trying to work out where Olsen goes, and how he gets there. He is relentlessly cultivating Murphy, whose loyalty to Olsen must surely crumble in the face of Hansen's wiles. So it won't be long before Olsen arrives to take his customary seat at the Jazz Theatre, only to find Hansen already there.

Claude and Bookie
Chichester Cathedral

'Ignorant people think it's the noise which fighting cats make that is so aggravating, but it ain't so; it's the sickening grammar they use'
Mark Twain

It's not so much that Claude and Bookie fight, but there is a certain tension between them. These two cats live with Nicholas Biddle, chaplain to the Bishop of Chichester, in a quiet corner of Canon Lane.

Before studying theology, Nicholas had been a choral scholar at Hereford Cathedral, where opportunity to observe the lives of cathedral cats was confined to fleeting glimpses of their rear quarters as they scaled the garden walls of the Bishop's Palace. But coming

THE CATHEDRAL

Described by the architectural historian Nicholas Pevsner as the most English of cathedrals, Chichester Cathedral was founded in 1075. It has been rebuilt at various times but retained a 14th century spire until its sudden collapse in 1861, miraculously without loss of life, and was rebuilt by the Victorian champion of restoration, Sir Gilbert Scott. Under the floor of the nave are the remains of a Roman mosaic pavement, which can be viewed through a glass window, and the cathedral also houses the grave of the composer Gustav Holst, and the Gothic 'Arundel tomb', famously referred to in Philip Larkin's poem.

Nicholas had been appointed Bishop's Chaplain, was doubly welcome. There would be less traffic nearby, and Claude would be free to wander, which he did with a vengeance. In the cloisters he discovered a black and white cat called Buggles, for whom Claude was a questionable addition to the attractions of Chichester Cathedral.

The irrepressible Claude turned Canon Lane into his personal playground, travelling from one end to the other by hopping from parked car to parked car. Nicholas can never work out how Claude always manages to leave a trail of muddy pawprints even on a perfectly dry day, and often a double set on cars that have been recently cleaned. Canon Lane was Claude's safe haven, somewhere to relax and unwind. One summer afternoon, he woke with a start to a hubbub of chatter and a clatter of boots as a large group of people walked through the lane. Two of the group pulled out guitars and began to sing and Claude, who has a problem with music at the

from a home where there were seven or eight cats at any given time, though, Nicholas was used to seeing cats in a somewhat calmer setting. When Nicholas went to take up a curacy in Bedford, he and his wife Marieke were joined by two cats, Claude and Minnie.

Having lost Minnie to local road traffic, a move to Chichester Cathedral, where best of times, stumped along the lane into the silence of his own home.

Claude was more than content to be the only household cat, and then Bookie, the last remaining cat of the Biddle feline clan (and at twenty-one this collection's oldest cat), arrived. Bookie had expected some sort of a welcome from Claude, some acknowledgement of his pre-eminence. But Claude forgot his manners, and completely ignored the new arrival. While Claude does his PR with the Bishop, Bookie sits, rather sullenly, behind the settee. There is an unspoken buffer zone between the two cats of several feet – up to thirty where space allows. There are no real confrontations, except the odd heartfelt but ineffective swat. Bookie has become a house cat, and spends much of his time in the study, from where he can gaze wistfully at the cathedral spire. Once in a while he wanders out, and is occasionally rewarded for his efforts by the sight of Claude being pursued by an indignant

Buggles, who is quite sure that the Bishop gave him sole right of access to the Palace gardens.

OPENING PAGE
The irrepressible Claude
LEFT
Bookie, the old family retainer
ABOVE
Claude does excellent PR with the Bishop

Godiva and Leofric
Durham Cathedral

'Cats, as a class, have never completely got over the snootiness caused by the fact that in Ancient Egypt they were worshipped as gods'
P.G. Wodehouse

Godiva and Leofric, the cathedral cats of Durham, live in one of the most spectacular settings in Britain with the Dean, Michael Sadgrove, and his family. The cathedral has been designated a UNESCO World Heritage Site, ranking it alongside such marvels as the pyramids and the Acropolis. Set high above the city in a loop of the River Wear, Durham Cathedral's distinctive twin towers and central tower can be seen for miles around, and in an autumnal light the whole building appears to emit a welcoming glow.

THE CATHEDRAL

This area played an important role in the early history of Christianity in Britain and Durham Cathedral houses the shrine of St Cuthbert (and fragments of his coffin) and the tomb of the Venerable Bede. The Lindisfarne Gospels once lived here too, but were removed by the King's Commissioners at the Reformation.

A large number of the original monastic buildings remain despite the depredations of the Reformation: the dormitory, refectory, (rebuilt) Chapter House, the Great Kitchen (now the cathedral bookshop) and the Deanery, formerly the prior's house.

On the day after their arrival in Durham Leofric disappeared. After a fruitless search for him around the house, gardens and the college green, the Sadgroves were at a loss. But that evening, the household was startled by unearthly sounds floating through the house; an extensive search suggested that these ghostly noises were coming from the depths of the Deanery, and Michael, poker in hand, and followed by some rather nervous children, descended into the cellars. The spectral howls grew louder as they passed into the monastic undercroft, until they eventually were tracked down to the iron grid covering the medieval latrine pit. At the sound of familiar voices the howls diminished into rather pathetic mews and Leofric, dishevelled, indignant and extremely hungry, was eventually extracted.

Not everyone was happy with the cats' arrival, especially the chapter clerk. With a notable lack of humility, however, the cats worked tirelessly to overcome this resistance, and the chapter clerk has now arranged for a cat-flap to be installed!

OPENING PAGE
Leofric and Godiva watch over College Green
LEFT
Leofric got lost in the medieval latrines
OPPOSITE RIGHT
Godiva on her way to a chapter house meeting

The initial encounter between Leofric and Godiva and the Archdeacon's cats exposed the fifteenth century cloisters to some fairly unecclesiastical language. In keeping with the studious and peaceful traditions of the cloisters, all the cats now avoid each other, each pair pretending that the other is invisible. Both Leofric and Godiva take their place in the twelfth century chapter house during meetings, and spend an inordinate amount of time seeking out the most comfortable laps. This inevitably delays the start of the meetings, as it is hard to concentrate on weighty matters when one has a cat circling and prodding endlessly on one's lap, trying to find exactly the right position. And why do cats always head for the person in black?

Winston, Wallace and Cassiopeia
St Mary's Episcopal Cathedral, Edinburgh

'The smallest feline is a masterpiece'
Leonardo de Vinci

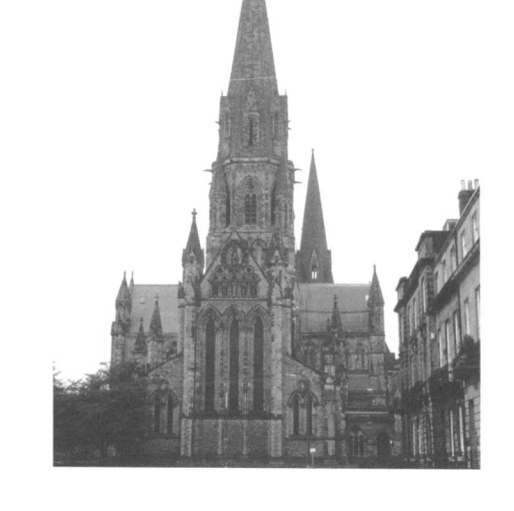

St Mary's Episcopal Cathedral sits imposingly at the centre of Palmerston Square, in Edinburgh's Georgian 'new town', the cathedral clergy and staff living nearby amidst understated Georgian elegance. Surrounded on all sides by roads, it does not seem an ideal place for cats. Yet there are some brave enough.

The Rev. Canon Jane Millard is Vice Provost of St Mary's and chaplain for the cathedral's important ministry to HIV sufferers. In the

THE CATHEDRAL

St Mary's Episcopal Cathedral is the youngest of the cathedrals featured in this book, and was the first cathedral to be built in the British Isles since the Reformation.

The cathedral's sandstone walls escaped the widespread sand-blasting of the 1980s, and so retain the same dark stonework appearance as the Walter Scott monument in Princes Street.

In the early days the Cathedral took part in the formation of an Industrial Dwelling Company to make affordable dwellings available for labourers. One of the cathedral's more prominent domestic activities these days is its mission to AIDS sufferers.

course of her work, she has helped to re-house more than thirty-three cats and thirty-two dogs. Winston was one of these: it became obvious after he had been re-housed that he was pining, so back he came. Winston wasn't too bothered by Jane's other cats, but to be in the house with two friendly dogs was a new experience, as Winston's previous encounters with canines had mainly involved high-speed escapes. He was fascinated. Every where the dogs went, so did Winston. He sampled their food, drank from their water, sat in their favourite places, and ultimately took over the dog basket. The poor dogs didn't know whether they were coming or going but eventually resigned themselves to a lifetime of Winston's too-close attentions.

The foundation of the cathedral is almost entirely owing to the generosity of Barbara and Mary Walker, who bequeathed their entire fortune to the Episcopalian Church, on the condition that a cathedral was built on their chosen site. Their interest has been taken over by Wallace and Cassiopeia, two cats who live by the cathedral in Palmerston Square. Wallace belongs to the Rev. William Mounsey, chaplain to the Royal Air Force at Leuchars, and Cassiopeia to the Rev. Dean

Fosterkew, Team Vicar at the cathedral. Wallace started out living by the airbase where William was chaplain, and loved the high octane Air Force life, delighting in being startled by the thunder of powerful jets and watching the aerobatics that were performed out over the sea. Upon the move to the more tranquil surroundings of St Mary's Cathedral Wallace was warmly welcomed by Cassiopeia, which was some kind of compensation.

Cassiopeia, a half Burmese, is a bit of a great-aunt cat, who spends much time tutting good-naturedly at the high spirits shown by the cathedral choristers as they pass on the way to the cathedral. She responds to all and sundry with a regal nod and, after she had explained the proper rules of conduct, Wallace eagerly joined her for the daily review of those passing, and responds to the choristers' cheerful greetings with an equally cheerful meow. When Wallace gets too familiar with people in the street, Cassiopeia

fusses him inside and reminds him of the cathedral cats' code of decorum.

OPENING PAGE

Winston won't let on whether it's milk or single malt in his 'Cuach'

LEFT

Wallace exchanged high-octane airforce life for the peace of St Mary's

ABOVE

Cassiopeia is the great-aunt cat

Hamish, Dilly, Suajeta, Scheherazade, Harry and Boots
Ely Cathedral

'One can pick a cat to fit almost any kind of decor, color, scheme, income, personality, mood'
Eric Gurney

Under the gaze of the unique octagonal tower of Ely Cathedral, its cathedral cats spend a lot of time in negotiation: all argue that they have legitimate claims to their territories, and concessions are reached only after extensive and noisy discussion. Ely Cathedral is home to a chorus of cats, all with their own particular territories.

The only things that can unite the Ely Cathedral cats are incursions by outside cats or a badly behaved dog. Hamish, a six-toed

THE CATHEDRAL
Known as the 'the ship of the Fens', Ely Cathedral dominates the flat fenland landscape. It was built on the site of a Saxon convent founded by Ethelreda; the present church was begun in the 11th century, with cathedral status being granted in 1109.

After the collapse of the original Norman central tower, Alan of Walsingham designed an octagonal tower, rather than a conventional four-sided one.

Cromwell used the cathedral to stable his cavalry, which may be why Ely Cathedral survived the Civil War relatively unscathed; but the dissolution of the monasteries and the Reformation took their toll, including the loss of St Ethelreda's much-visited shrine.

ginger fellow, lives with the verger, Martin Fleet, his wife Paula, and their two children. Next to them lives the cathedral Bursar, Stephen Wikner and his wife Stefanie, with their two cats Boots and Harry. It is this domestic proximity that has originated intense on-going feline discussions about land rights. The territory under dispute takes in the largest collection of medieval buildings still in domestic use: the Chapter House, Powcher's Hall and the Black Hostelry (so named after the black habits worn by the Benedictine monks). The Ely Cathedral cats range without hindrance from the Great Gateway (at one time a gaol and, more recently, an ale-house), through the King's School grounds, the Dean's Meadow and Ely Park and, further away, down to the banks of the River Great Ouse.

Dilly, Scheherazade and Suajeta live with their family, the Porter-Thaws, around the other side of the cathedral, in what is now the Choir House: they avoid the more rumbustious areas inhabited by Harry et al., preferring the cover afforded by the old monastic buildings and cathedral offices. These are the laid-back cats of Ely, who prefer to flop around listening to music, hanging out with choristers and music students. Hamish, Harry and Boots, on the other hand, have all tried to get in, and have been summarily ejected from the Porter-Thaws' garden. There have been accidental encounters, as when all the cats converged unintentionally at the Galilee Porch (a fine example of Early English architecture). This noisy affair was dealt with in a firm but fair manner by the vigilant vergers, who had already dealt with one cat emergency – Harry had been accidentally locked in, and spent an unhappy night curled up near the stone slab marking the place where St Etheldreda's shrine stood. He has now forsworn the cathedral and has taken to mooching around by the river; it remains to be seen what he makes of the swans.

Emma and Thomas
Exeter Cathedral

'I believe cats to be spirits come to earth. A cat,
I am sure, could walk on a cloud without
coming through'
Jules Verne

Whether the nursery rhyme 'Hickory
Dickory Dock' really did have its origins at
Exeter Cathedral is disputable, but the 15th
century astronomical clock in the North
Transept does have some interesting
features: built by a Glastonbury monk, the
workings of this clock would have been
greased with animal fat – particularly
appetizing to mice. In the doorway that gives
access to the clock there is a crude hole,
reputedly made to give access to a cat in hot
pursuit of these horological rodents! And

THE CATHEDRAL
Exeter Cathedral was built in the Romanesque style
by William the Conqueror's nephew William
Warelwast, but underwent substantial reconstruction
in the 13th century.

The cathedral has had a turbulent history,
beginning with the damage inflicted by the
besieging forces of King Stephen in 1136, via the
demolition of the cloisters under Cromwell, to a
direct hit from a German bomb during one of the
so-called 'Baedeker raids'. Under the Parliamen-
tarian governor Colonel Hammond, the cathedral
had to be partitioned by a brick wall in order to allow
Presbyterian and Congregationalist congregations to
worship at the same time.

bride and groom were vets, and during the reception engaged Neil in a lengthy conversation about their need to re-house an amiable stray ginger tomcat. On arriving home, Canon Collings consulted Joan, his cat sitter, as to whether Emma would mind another cat. She thought a ginger cat might be a fine companion; Emma was very maternal and would welcome the opportunity to use her motherly traits. And so it proved, with the cats developing a relationship rather like that of AA Milne's Kanga and Tigger – maternal and calm versus irrepressible and bouncy. The two cats had formed an enduring friendship by the time they came to Exeter Cathedral, where

medieval archives show that there was a cat on the cathedral staff, who received a weekly payment of one penny.

Thomas came into Canon Neil Collings's life as a result of a wedding he presided over during his time as a vicar in Harpenden. The

Neil became Canon Treasurer. It was Advent Sunday when they all arrived at the late fourteenth century Canon's house overlooking the Cathedral green. Thomas and Emma spent the first few days creeping around anxiously, but in due course they relaxed.

Thomas acquired a circle of admirers who would make a point of coming to see him, and he was transformed into a rumbustious dandy. He was swept away by all the adulation and he set out to bring the message of his glorious felinity wide and far. Not all paths lead home, and one particular promenade took him out into the swirl of the High Street, and there he got lost. A frantic search discovered a slightly chastened Thomas a few days later, at the Exeter Cats Protection League. For a while he was chastened, but with the news of his adventure a local newspaper published his photograph, and there was a postcard of him on sale in the cathedral bookshop: he was

soon back to his old ways. Inside the house, though, Thomas plays to the gallery in a different way, feigning such helplessness that Emma, brushing aside her irritation at his public antics, still mothers and fusses around him, as though he were still the bouncy but vulnerable cat that first came to the vicarage at Harpenden.

Bonnie and Flora
Gloucester Cathedral

'A cat's got her own opinion of human beings. She don't say much, but you can tell enough to make you anxious not to hear the whole of it'
Jerome K. Jerome

There is a great tradition of cats in Gloucester. Dick Wittington's cat is supposed to have come from here, and legend has it that all the cats of the city speak to each other on Christmas Eve. The cathedral also has a lively tradition of resident cats: Gorbachov, featured in the first Cathedral Cats book, who was succeeded by Maud, who in turn handed over the post to Bonnie.

Canon residentiary David Hoyle came to Gloucester about two years ago, with his wife

THE CATHEDRAL

Gloucester Cathedral is a beacon of history and heritage in a city that, courtesy of the 1960s, is otherwise a nightmare of concrete. Construction of the present building began in the late 11th century, and despite fires, the collapse of the Southern tower and the uncertainties of civil war, the building was in generally good repair by the time of the coronation at the cathedral of Henry III, in 1216.

Edward II's burial at Gloucester after his murder helped it escape the excesses of Henry VIII's dissolution of the monasteries, given his respect for his ancestor's tomb. Pilgrims visiting the tomb partly financed the perpendicular-style choir and presbytery.

Janet, daughter Katy and Bonnie the cat. Bonnie had led a settled life in London, and didn't take at all kindly to being relocated: within a very short while of arriving, she moved out. Despite a thorough and persistent search, there was no sign of her; she simply vanished, and after a month Katy had given up hope of ever seeing Bonnie again.

In the meantime, Janet Hoyle's sister Helen had come to live with them in the cathedral close, bringing with her a wide-eyed and jumpy black and white cat by the name of Flora. Flora took to life at the cathedral with even less enthusiasm than Bonnie; at the first opportunity she fled into a maze of medieval cellars and drains beneath the house. In the end, after a lot of cajoling, pleading, and possibly just a little prodding, Flora re-emerged into daylight.

One afternoon, Katy made her way to a friend's home, where, on the window sill, looking a bit shamefaced but in very good shape, was Bonnie. After a slightly tense reunion, Bonnie was returned to her rightful owner, only to find that her place had apparently been taken by another cat who was nothing more than a bag of nerves. Bonnie wasn't having this, and at the first opportunity she wandered off again, and moved in with another local family. It was the verger's ginger cat Tinker who sorted things out. He pointed out to her some of the many advantages of life as a cathedral cat, not the least of which were the tidbits that could be cadged from unwary visitors. Bonnie relented, returning home for a reconciliation with her family.

Tinker's advice was sound; Bonnie found that people regularly come to eat a snack lunch in the calm of the cathedral close, and though clearly far from being malnourished, she developed a piteous miaow alongside her rampant appetite for chips. Inside the cathedral, Bonnie regularly sits on David Hoyle's knees during evensong, cocking a critical ear at the choir, and joins official processions (graciously permitting the Bishop to walk in front of her). The only

thing likely to send her running for home is the sonorous booming of Great Peter, Britain's only remaining medieval bell, as it rings out over the city.

OPENING PAGE
Bonnie strikes a pose
OPPOSITE LEFT
Bonnie is now a consummate performer
ABOVE
Flora had no interest in being rescued from the cellars

Saffron and Mevagissey
Hereford Cathedral

'It always gives me a shiver when I see a cat seeing what I can't see'

Eleanor Farjeon

Saffron and Mevagissey arrived in this world in unusual circumstances. Their parents, Cable and Wireless, had been taken for neutering at four months; the only problem was that one of them, Wireless, was already pregnant. The two kittens were given to Peter Dyke, the assistant cathedral organist, and installed in the cloister house.

There are two cloisters at Hereford Cathedral: the Bishop's Cloister, which is open to the public, and the College

THE CATHEDRAL

The rose-coloured sandstone of Hereford Cathedral is in harmony with the red soil of this traditionally farming-centred county. Like so many cathedrals, it has been rebuilt to various extents at different times, and has known both good times and bad in tandem with the rise and fall of the diocese's power and influence.

Never a monastic establishment, for the best part of twelve centuries the cathedral here has comprised three main elements: the church; its library; and its school. Today, two of Britain's most important historical treasures, the Mappa Mundi and Chained Library, are proudly displayed in the new library at Hereford.

Cloisters, so called because they originally housed the Vicar's Choral, who sang in the cathedral choir.

The two cats have inherited a large area of the cathedral precincts from their predecessor Princess, to which they have added the Bishop's Palace Gardens, the deanery, and a vast swathe of lawn running down to the River Wye.

The West Front of the cathedral, however, is unknown to the cats: the close has proved to be the most hazardous area of the cathedral for Saffron and Mevagissey, as they have had to run the gauntlet of the gimlet-eyed dog belonging to the cathedral organist, Dr Roy Massey. This is a time-honoured tradition of feline life at Hereford Cathedral. The cats do not like the rush and bustle of Broad Street so visits to the new cathedral library building, which houses the world-famous Mappa Mundi and chained library, are off the agenda.

The scaffolding on the Lady Chapel has provided Saffron with endless hours of fun, as has a large yew tree: visitors and staff are often startled by the ghostly vision of two white cats stretched out along its branches, inscrutably surveying their domain. These cats do get around; they seem to have a window fixation. At a year old Saffron wandered off, and was found living on the third floor of the Deanery, under a bed, and even now often clambers into the adjacent verger's house through an upstairs bedroom window.

Domestic life has its dramas too. The cats' house in the cloisters has an extra and uninvited occupant: the ghost of one John Constable, butler to the college, who died in mysterious circumstances. Saffron and Mevagissey have been frequently startled by locked windows suddenly rushing open, and by the unexplained banging of doors. Ghosts apart, home life is entertaining: as a kitten Mevagissey liked to sleep inside the grand piano, on the strings. Only a vigorous exercise in chromatic scales would dislodge

their strings (thankfully unaware that they are made from cat gut!).

Saffron and Mevagissey have no established routine for casual visits; the only place that receives their regular attention is the office of the Cathedral Perpetual Trust, where food is set out in anticipation; but even then they won't enter through the door, only a window. The only rooms that Saffron and Mevagissey enter via the door are those in their own house, and committee meeting rooms, where they will follow Peter or Shaun, looking around for a lap to sit on, preferably belonging to someone wearing sombre black, so as to show off to best effect the white hairs they leave!

her, and she still sits gazing in fascination at the rise and fall of the hammers, putting out a tentative exploratory paw every now and then. Saffron prefers the collection of period string instruments scattered about the house, and occasionally takes a tentative pluck at

Kim and Boris
Lichfield Cathedral

'To respect the cat is the beginning of the aesthetic sense'

Erasmus Darwin

A close examination of the cathedral staff photo at Lichfield Cathedral reveals, peering out from between the feet of cathedral groundsman Mark Jervis, a wiry and determined-looking grey cat. This is Kim, unofficial sovereign of Lichfield Cathedral, and official cathedral cat.

Inside the cathedral there is a handsome memorial to Darwin, and the city's intellectual traditions are also handsomely acknowledged by memorials to Samuel

THE CATHEDRAL

Lichfield Cathedral's three distinctive spires are instantly recognizable, as are the ranks of carved figures that ornament the cathedral's west front, and the city's intellectual traditions are handsomely acknowledged by memorials to Samuel Johnson, David Garrick and Erasmus Darwin.

The first church here was a Saxon cathedral, built by Bishop Hedda in 700, to house the remains of St Chad.

Lichfield Cathedral lost its status as a see after the Norman invasion, but an early Norman bishop, Roger de Clinton, rebuilt the cathedral, fortified the close and provided renewed facilities for pilgrims.

OPENING PAGE
Kim waits for the bishop
LEFT
**Kim, always under-awed
by her surroundings**
OPPOSITE RIGHT
**Boris comes off the
night shift**

Johnson and David Garrick. As befits a
cathedral that stands in a city celebrated by
Daniel Defoe for its 'good conversation and
good company', Lichfield Cathedral takes its
place in a thoroughly contemporary manner
at the heart of the annual Lichfield Music
Festival, during which its imposing nave
echoes with an eclectic and inspiring series
of concerts, recitals and performances. But
this means little to Kim, who is a true one-

person cat, with strict limits on the time she has available for visitors. Kim is a pure-bred farm cat, born among the rough and tumble of sheepdogs and livestock, and there is little that she needs to be taught about survival: Kim rules the cathedral close with claws of iron, acting as if Lichfield Cathedral was an extensive farm, with one particularly large and ornate barn.

Boris, her so-called companion, is a simpler soul. He came as company for Kim, despite Kim's objections. After countless protracted and vigorous disputes about food, bedding, which entrance to use, where each cat was allowed to go, which cat got to lie in front of the fire and who got to sit on Mark's lap, an exhausted and exasperated Mark calmed the situation by devising a shift system. Boris was sent out for the night shift, patrolling the cathedral close, and doing all the unmentionable things that cats do at night; he comes back to the house after breakfast. Kim got the day shift – which fitted with the

routine she had already established: she leaves the house through the front door at the exact moment Boris comes in through the front window. The only continuing source of disagreement between the two cats now is whether it is permitted for Boris to sleep on Kim's cushion and vice versa. Perversely each cat insists on sleeping on the other's bedding.

Setting aside the complications of domestic life, Kim has another curious trait: she is the feline equivalent of a working dog, displaying a dog-like loyalty to Mark, trotting at his heels round the grounds and through the cathedral: she comes to a whistle (which she can hear over a quarter of a mile), and she keeps livestock in check – by which one is understood to refer to visiting dogs. What Kim lacks in size is more than made up for in determination and the ability to surprise. Even large dogs flinch when they hear a rustling in the lavender bushes beside the path, and small dogs leap quivering into their owners' arms. Not that Kim is unnecessarily violent – she just likes to run a tight ship, and dogs, well... dogs are untidy. I imagine that no animals are involved at the childrens' Christmas crib ceremonies – any donkey with an ounce of sense would know that it would be courting disaster to disturb Kim from an afternoon rest in the crib.

There are a few choice friends that Kim visits: she often calls into to see Pauline Hawkins in the cathedral offices (which just happen to be next to the cathedral coffee shop). But more often than not, Kim can be seen sitting behind Mark, on a small tractor, like one of those sheep dogs in a farm trailer that one follows endlessly down twisting country lanes.

LEFT

Kim on dog patrol

RIGHT

From time to time Kim checks that Boris is not sleeping in her bed

Ivor
Portsmouth Cathedral

'It is difficult to obtain the friendship of a cat. It is a philosophical animal … one that does not place its affections thoughtlessly'

Théophile Gautier

Ivor, a genial white and ginger cat with an unusual retroussé nose, lives in a pleasantly ramshackle Georgian house next to Portsmouth cathedral with the cathedral organist David Price and his wife Kitty. Although Ivor was born on a farm, he turned out more of a meals-on-wheels cat than a farm-bred kitten.

Ivor's home overlooks the east end of the cathedral, and from the first floor there is a fine view of the eleventh century chancel and

THE CATHEDRAL

Portsmouth Cathedral has been a place of worship for sea-farers since it was first built, and until 1828 naval officers taking up their first command were required to take communion here.

The cathedral is based around the original chapel of St Thomas of Canterbury which was built in 1170 by a Norman land-owner, Jean de Gisor, features of which are still visible in the present cathedral.

The town's inhabitants were excommunicated and the church closed in the 15th century when local sailors murdered the Bishop of Chichester. The Civil War also took its toll – its tower doubled as a lighthouse and lookout and was an obvious target for Parliamentary gunners.

transept, surmounted by a tower with a distinctive wooden cupola. For a year Ivor couldn't be bothered to go out, but one day he spotted Daisy, a neighbouring lady cat of apparently easy virtue. After only the briefest of encounters, Daisy dumped Ivor, but the episode had served to get Ivor out of the house, and he now started to take a more active interest in cathedral goings-on. Initial visits were confined to the cathedral offices, housed in a cloister-like corridor on the north side of the cathedral, where Ivor was regularly entertained by the cathedral administrator Tom Morton, Commodore RN (rtd) and his tales of life on the high seas. From here it was a short stroll to the vergers' office, where Ivor initiated a regular series of lengthy discussions with the vergers, usually on the topic of what was in the vergers' well-stocked refrigerator, and would they mind if he took a peek?

Eventually Ivor found his way into the cathedral, where one of his first acts was to

OPENING PAGE
Ivor tries out a new voluntary
ABOVE
The Bishop's chair makes a good vantage point

other cathedral activities, which he clearly regards as an important part of his official responsibilities.

LEFT
A chat with the vergers is always welcome
BELOW
A rummage around the font is the nearest that Ivor can get to a dry dock

test out the acoustics, now a regular activity for him; to their credit, the good folk who worship here don't bat an eyelid when their prayers and contemplations are punctuated by a series of plaintive miaows, usually in the key of A minor. Ivor also found a great position from which to observe the daily rounds of cathedral life – the comfort of the William and Mary Bishop's Chair. Around this time Ivor also started to go out of the house to greet the cathedral choristers, whom he now regularly accompanies to evensong. From choral singing it was a short leap to joining in childrens' workshops and

Samson and Delilah
Ripon Cathedral

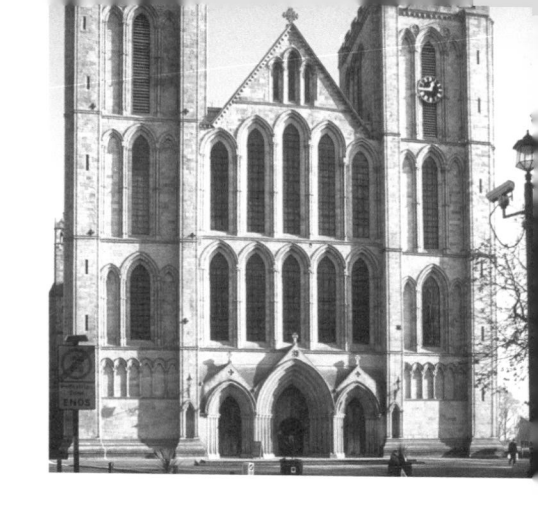

'It is a very inconvenient habit of kittens that,
whatever you say to them, they always purr'
Lewis Carroll

Samson and Delilah, the family cats of John
Methuen, the Dean of Ripon, and his wife
Bridgit, pointedly ignore the Dean's claim to
be more of a dog person than a cat person.
Delilah, the bolder of the two cats, leads
regular incursions into the Dean's study,
particularly when there are visitors or
meetings, and plants herself emphatically in
the centre of the room, from which position
she looks around as if to say 'What are you
going to do about it?'. In the event, the Dean
does nothing, and can frequently be seen

THE CATHEDRAL
Possibly the most striking aspect of Ripon Cathedral
is the newly-restored Early English West Front – the
sandstone used in its construction gives it a
welcoming glow. The original church of St Peter was
built in the seventh century by St Wilfrid, and the
crypt is still preserved under the medieval minster.
The present church building is the fourth to occupy
the site, and became the cathedral church of the
diocese of Ripon in 1836.

An extensive collection of misericords and carved
bench ends includes the famous 'rabbit hole' miseri-
cord, which is claimed to have played a part in inspiring Lewis Carroll, son of a residentiary canon of
the cathedral, to write *Alice's Adventures in Wonderland*.

with a cat on his lap, looking pretty relaxed – for a man who prefers dogs.

Samson and Delilah originally arrived with the Methuens' daughter, who was in transit for London, and the family decided that life would be safer for the kittens at Ripon. The same daughter's London home includes a German Shepherd and a Doberman who come to visit at Ripon, and although Samson and Delilah are politely hospitable, they are not too upset when it is time for the dogs to bounce back to London.

With nothing much to worry them inside the house, the cats sought adventure further afield. The wall separating the Deanery garden and cathedral churchyard was easily climbed from the garden, but there was rather more of a drop on the cathedral side,

and even after some time Samson would only go as far as the top of the wall. Delilah, on the other hand, was eager to explore the 'far side'. Her wanderings were normally restricted to the churchyard, but one cold winter's afternoon, Delilah's curiosity led her to the West door of the cathedral, and as a late visitor came out, she slipped in.

Avoiding the attention of the vergers, Delilah made her way up the nave, passing through the fifteenth century pulpitum into the chancel, where a choir practice was in progress. The organist noticed that the choristers were not concentrating: the younger members kept breaking into fits of giggles. Peering down, the organist spotted Delilah, alternately winding her way through the choristers' legs, and hopping along the choir stalls. The organist reached for a lever that operated a 17th century mechanical hand, used in days gone by to conduct the choir from the organ loft. This caught Delilah's attention: she gazed up nervously at

this disembodied hand, creaking up and down with increasing vigour, and after one particularly wild and clattering gesture, her nerve broke, and Delilah beat a hasty retreat. Once outside, she tore past a startled Samson and tumbled back over the wall into the safety of the deanery. And that was that. Both cats prowl the Deanery gardens, and Delilah mooches around the churchyard, but there is no way she is ever going to face the phantom hand of Ripon Cathedral again.

Figaro
Rochester Cathedral

'What greater gift than the love of a cat?'
Charles Dickens

Rochester Cathedral stands between the old Roman Watling Street (now Rochester High Street), the imposing Norman castle and the old Roman Wall. The strategic position of the town on the River Medway made it a scene of conflict from the times of the Viking invasions through to the Civil War and the cathedral suffered heavy damage from fire on several occasions.

The Norman archbishop Gundulf was charged with the rebuilding of Rochester

THE CATHEDRAL

The second oldest cathedral foundation in England, Rochester Cathedral has survived successive conflicts and fire.

At the Dissolution, the priory was the last monastic house to submit to the Royal Commissioners, and Henry VIII, having appropriated the priory buildings as a royal palace, appointed the last prior as the first Dean of the cathedral.

The 18th century saw construction of houses within the precincts, settings often used in the novels of Charles Dickens, and following further restorations by the Victorian architect Sir George Gilbert Scott, the cathedral has, for the last century or so, enjoyed a welcome period of tranquillity.

Figaro has a superb territory, taking in the King's Gardens, the cloister garth and the Deanery garden, as well as nearby Minor Canon Row, and straying into the Dickensian cobbled lanes that criss-cross the nearby High Street. Canon Jonathan Meyrick (Acting Dean of the cathedral) and his family came to Rochester from a rural parish in Wiltshire, where animals were a dominant feature of domestic life. One can't help but see Jonathan Meyrick as a sort of David Attenborough of cathedral life.

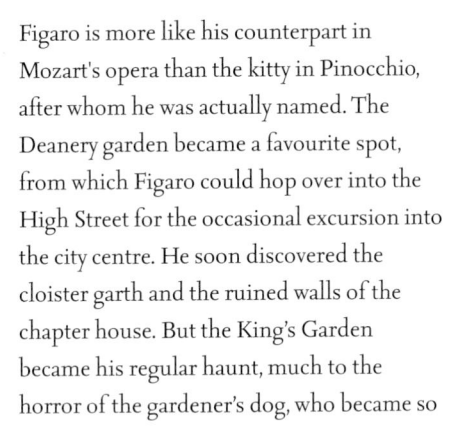

Figaro is more like his counterpart in Mozart's opera than the kitty in Pinocchio, after whom he was actually named. The Deanery garden became a favourite spot, from which Figaro could hop over into the High Street for the occasional excursion into the city centre. He soon discovered the cloister garth and the ruined walls of the chapter house. But the King's Garden became his regular haunt, much to the horror of the gardener's dog, who became so

Cathedral, and this may account for the survival of much of the original Romanesque architecture, for Gundulf founded the Tower of London and the nearby Rochester Castle. There are still some traces of original Roman brickwork in the nearby city walls, and notably in the footings of the walls of the ruined Chapter House, a favourite vantage point of Figaro, the Rochester Cathedral cat.

nervous that he flinched every time a leaf blew across the lawn.

Back at home there was a shock in store. In Jonathan Meyrick's study there is a large heated glass tank, with a secure cover that Figaro likes to perch on. He wasn't much interested in the contents, then one day, he saw something move – or slither, rather – under a piece of wood. Alerted, Figaro hopped down and sat, nose pressed to the glass, waiting for further signs of movement. He sat and waited patiently, as only cats can do. After about half an hour he began to lose interest; he looked around, had a bit of a wash, and turned back to the glass tank, whereupon he found, gazing at him intently, a large snake. Figaro's life flashed before his eyes. Fur on end, he hurtled up the curtains, and there remained for quite a while. From that point on, Figaro was reformed. He even made a point of befriending the gardener's dog, and welcomed back into the cathedral gardens all the wild life that had

previously moved out. He has eventually become accustomed to Cleo, and sits outside her snake house, extending a (very) tentative paw to pat the glass if she emerges from hiding.

OPENING PAGE
Cat, camouflaged
OPPOSITE LEFT
There are still some unresolved issues with local cats
ABOVE
Figaro, recovering from meeting Cleo, the snake

Wolfie
Salisbury Cathedral

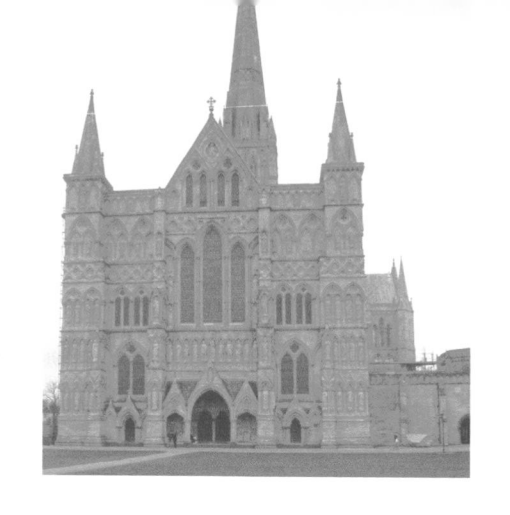

'Of all God's creatures, there is only one that cannot be made slave of the leash. That one is the cat. If man could be crossed with the cat it would improve the man, but it would deteriorate the cat'
Mark Twain

Celebrated in paintings by Joseph Turner and John Constable, Salisbury Cathedral is one of the most recognisable buildings in Britain, a unique example of unified Early English architecture. Salisbury Cathedral also takes its cats very seriously.

The extent of the residential close perhaps explains the proliferation of cats here. Wolfie first came to the cathedral as a kitten, and lived with Canon June Osborne, who had recently been appointed Dean of Salisbury

THE CATHEDRAL

Salisbury Cathedral is a unique example of unified Early English architecture. Built on foundations of no more than one and a half metres, on a water meadow, the cathedral has the tallest spire in Britain. The octagonal spire was added about a hundred years after the first stone was laid, and has remained secure despite a pronounced lean at the top.

One of the treasures of the cathedral is an ancient clock mechanism dating from 1386 and said to be the oldest piece of machinery still at work in Britain, if not the entire world.

Anthony Trollope set many of his novels in and around the cathedral, notably *The Warden* and *Barchester Towers*.

Cathedral. After six months, though, Wolfie turned his back on a caring household. Some cats are naturally nomadic, and my guess is that he couldn't resist the allure of the cathedral, with its wide-open spaces and friendly population. (To this day, though, the Dean remains Wolfie's official kin, paying for his veterinary care and upkeep, lucky cat.)

But it was not in Wolfie's stars to be a stray: he put in regular appearances in the cloisters, which the cathedral somehow acquired in the middle of the 13th century, despite never having been a monastic establishment. Their tranquillity belies the existence behind them of an extremely busy and industrious cathedral works department. And here Wolfie hung his hat, so to speak. The craftsmen of the works department have a well-established interest in cats; Ginger, now immortalized in a stained glass window depicting the laying of the original foundation stone of the

OPENING PAGE
Wolfie casts a critical eye over the stonemasons' work

RIGHT
The cloisters, one of Wolfie's many cathedral haunts

OPPOSITE RIGHT
Waiting for Steve Mellor and Sunday roast chicken

cathedral, was a stoneyard resident. Wolfie took up residence, and for a while was looked after by the cathedral glaziers, whom he would follow up scaffolding and ladders, looking for all the world like a furry black gargoyle come to life.

Wolfie has also colonised the cathedral itself, slipping into the south aisle from the cloisters, or wailing pitifully by the south transept door until let in by a visitor. Fortunately for Wolfie, the tolerance threshold for cats is particularly high at Salisbury. Wolfie once turned up to an early morning Eucharist, where he sat by the server's chair on the right of the celebrant, gazing at the Dean. Then when the Dean went up to read the Gospel, Wolfie went too, sitting by the Dean while he read.

Wolfie is now cared for by Steve Mellor of the works department. He feeds Wolfie every day of the year, with roast chicken for Sunday lunch, and he doesn't take holidays anymore, as he'd rather be with Wolfie. And what does Steve get in return? Well, as the author William S. Burroughs put it: 'The cat offers itself. Of course he wants care and shelter. You don't buy love for nothing. Like all pure creatures, cats are practical.'

Jasper and Eddie
Southwell Minster

*'Cats are smarter than dogs. You can't get eight
cats to pull a sled through snow'*
Jeff Valdez

The cats of Southwell Minster live with
Richard Davey, Residentiary Canon, his wife
Sam and their daughter Caitlin. The Daveys
previously spent four years at St Edmundsbury, where Richard would walk around the
churchyard with their black and white cat
Sylvester, fending off the not entirely well-
intentioned advances of Daisy and Lazarus
(see St Edmundsbury Cathedral).

When Jasper, a little white kitten from a cat
rescue centre, was added to the Davey

THE CATHEDRAL

Southwell Minster nestles comfortably into its semi-
rural surroundings, modestly signalling its existence
with two distinctive 'pepperpot' spires. The Saxon
Minster church was established by Oskytel,
Archbishop of York, towards the latter part of the
eighth century.

Towards the end of the 1200s, Southwell acquired
the Chapter House, which was originally decorated
in vivid colours: it is a riot of carvings, depicting
animals, plants, trees and fruits, all of which
probably served as a very early form of visual aid to a
largely illiterate congregation. In 1884, the Minster
acquired its present status as cathedral for the newly
created Southwell diocese.

OPENING PAGE
A deaf Jasper and an earth-bound Eddie
BELOW
Although deaf, Jasper tracks the dogs through vibration
OPPOSITE RIGHT
Eddie reflects on the problems of flight

menagerie, there was widespread outrage – but all the wailing and squawking had no effect on Jasper, since he is deaf. Jasper's initial outings were secular: he had a favourite pub close to the cathedral, and started to show signs of wanting to visit the nearby brewery but a protesting Jasper was confined to quarters. Perhaps that was why the Daveys were relieved to move to Southwell Minster, a peaceful contrast to the bustle of Bury St Edmunds.

Their newfound peace did not last long: the arrival of Max, Fen and Hal (collie, lurcher and whippet puppies respectively) ensured that Jasper and Sylvester were kept on their paws. The three dogs did nothing but rush around the house, gobbling up the cat food and barging into rooms uninvited. Without hearing, Jasper was nonetheless able track the dogs from the vibrations of wagging tails beating against doors and walls, and the scrabbling of paws on the wooden and stone floors. Sylvester nosed the dogs' food dishes

into a narrow space by the washing machine. With the dogs sugbjugated, Sylvester was free to settle into semi-retirement, by which time another cat had arrived – Eddie.

When Sylvester died, Eddie was given his collar, confirming his seniority in the animal hierarchy of the household. To tell the truth, he wasn't very good at it, getting involved in some rather questionable adventures. In short, Eddie lived up to his name – which he had taken from Eddie the Eagle, an amiable but catastrophic ski-jumper. He was determined to emulate his namesake's spectacular but misjudged airborne antics. One evening, Eddie got so carried away that he launched himself from the top of a tree into thin air. To his surprise, flapping his paws didn't really work, and he landed in a spread-eagled pile beside a startled verger. Learning from experience isn't one of Eddie's strong points: he persisted in his flight experiments, undeterred even by a bad landing on ice which broke his pelvis.

Both he and Jasper have great fun scratching marks into the trees that line the Minster churchyard, a type of feline mason's mark that echoes the marks of the original stone masons that are scattered throughout Southwell Minster.

Adam and Florence
Westminster Abbey

'If animals could speak the dog would be a blundering outspoken fellow, but the cat would have the rare grace of never saying a word too much'

Mark Twain

Although Westminster Abbey is not a cathedral, this 'House of Kings' has a unique place in the history of Britain. There are many cats living at the abbey, and a fair few who just pass through. Many of these make their way through the home ground of Adam and Florence, who live with the Very Rev. Canon David Hutt in a secluded Georgian house overlooking the College Garden.

By the twelfth century, the Abbey at Westminster had become a thriving centre of

THE CATHEDRAL

Despite being in the heart of London, Westminster Abbey manages to keep its distance from the noise, rush and swirl of urban life.

Edward the Confessor built the original Benedictine Abbey at Westminster. By the 12th century, the Abbey had become a thriving centre of pilgrimage to his tomb.

When Elizabeth I refounded the abbey, the original monastic community was replaced by a dean and chapter, and in 1560 was constituted as a 'Royal Peculiar', accountable only to the Sovereign. There are monarchs, politicians, warriors, scientists, musicians and poets all buried here.

pilgrimage to the tomb of Edward the Confessor, with the monastic community dividing their duties between prayer, maintenance of the Abbey and caring for the pilgrims. The well-tended College Garden, probably the oldest in England, has been looked after continuously for over 900 years.

It was originally a source of medicinal herbs, as well as a source of food, and hyssop and fennel still grow here, much to the interest of the cats, who frequently stand by the fennel, noses raised and eyes shut. The garden is now used for special events, and has recently been opened to the public, and Adam and Florence have exploited this to the full – David has been sent photographs of the cats in the garden by captivated visitors from all over the world. Adam did once manage to climb one of the trees, but getting down was another thing altogether, and the gardeners embarked on a rescue mission. Better scrambling areas are provided by the fourteenth century stone precinct walls that bound part of the garden.

Summer is a time for visiting neighbours: both cats set out quite early, exchanging relatively polite greetings with Denis, the verger's cat who lives nearby. In fact Denis is usually on his way to David Hutt's house for a second breakfast, while Florence, with the

OPENING PAGE

Florence: a dignified cat in august surroundings

ABOVE

Off for a second breakfast with the verger

OPPOSITE RIGHT

Adam likes ice and an olive in his cocktails

same object in mind, is making for Denis's residence. Adam normally makes do with only the one meal to start his day, and then strolls over to the cloisters, and thence to Dean's Yard, where he passes the time of day with visitors and abbey staff – if only he could pick up David's mail for him! Adam is a water and ice cat: he'll sit for hours by the pool in the Little Cloister, watching the water from the central fountain falling back, taking an occasional drink, every now and again dipping a paw. At home the sounds of running water, or of tinkling ice in a glass always bring him running; when the fridge is defrosted he hooks out some of the ice, and whacks it like a hockey puck around the house. He gets a bit confused when the ice melts, but then we can't all be scientists. This fascination for ice draws Adam to any cocktail party going. That and olives, which both cats go for in a big way.

Then there are various fund-raising and special events that take place in the garden.

As a 'Royal Peculiar' the Abbey is accountable only to the Sovereign, and is the setting for a variety of glittering events. All coronations since 1066 – save two – have taken place here, and numerous other royal and state

occasions as well. Life is put into perspective when one sees, among the splendour of ceremonial uniforms, ecclesiastical regalia and extravagant garden party hats, Adam and Florence, two most ordinary cats wandering around, perfectly at home with the great and the good.

Marmaduke, Fatcat and PJ
Worcester Cathedral

'Cats are intended to teach us that not everything in nature has a purpose'
Garrison Keillor

Worcester Cathedral is set in an idyllic position on the banks of the River Severn, where it has become an accidental icon for that most English of pastimes, cricket! After Bishop Wulfstan's canonization, the cathedral became an ever more popular centre of pilgrimage, and King John was buried within it.

By the beginning of the fifteenth century, Worcester Cathedral was much as it is today. The cathedral is still surrounded by small

THE CATHEDRAL

Worcester Cathedral boasts a magnificent architecture and rich history. It was the site, in 1717, of the first Three Choirs Festival, which continues to this day.

Inside today's cathedral can be found a plaque commemorating 'Woodbine Willy', a battlefront chaplain during the Great War who handed out copies of the New Testament together with packs of cigarettes. A more famous son of Worcester is the composer Sir Edward Elgar, remembered in the magnificent 'Gerontius' stained-glass window close to the north door.

remnants of the Benedictine monastery, which combine with the remains of the cloister and the walled gardens to create a quadrangle giving the cathedral close, or College Green, as it is now known, the intimate air of an Oxford college.

Marmaduke, a portly and genial ginger cat, lives in a secluded corner of College Green with the cathedral organist Adrian Lucas, his wife Joanna and their children Hannah and William. The household is a highly musical one, with a steady flow of students taking lessons, as well as Adrian's own musical activities and preparations, Marmaduke doesn't care to listen to much; he pleads urgent business elsewhere. On one occasion Marmaduke was in such a hurry to get out of earshot that he scampered up the steps into College Hall to find himself in the midst of some eighty students just starting a Maths A-level exam. Spying an empty chair, he sat down quietly, trying to avoid the eagle-eyed invigilators; but, alas, he was spotted, and being unable to produce his candidate number, was politely but firmly escorted out.

Music is impossible to avoid at Worcester Cathedral, so for music-eschewing Marmaduke the rule is: never go near the cathedral during the Three Choirs Festival or

PJ, watched over by Fate
**The amiable Marmaduke
beams a welcome**
**Fat Cat, who really wants
to be a duck**

in the late afternoon (evensong), on Sunday mornings, or on any of the other days (and there are many) when there are recitals or other concerts. In order to keep himself music-free, Marmaduke generally confines his cathedralic appearances to the cloisters and the gift shop.

At the other end of the college green, by the medieval gatehouse that leads into College Green, live Canon Alvyn Pettersen and his family. They came to Worcester from Frensham, where daughter Catherine busied herself creating a miniature farm (she describes herself as a 'farmer in the making'). Consequently, the peace of College Green is sometimes disturbed by barking, clucking, quacking, the hoarse call of a harassed rooster, and the occasional meow from a cat called, perhaps somewhat unkindly, FatCat. FatCat is another rescue cat, and has to bear the indignity of being named differently by each member of the family – she is known variously as FatCat, Pirelli, Humbug and Schmuck, but the variation doesn't matter as all of these names is equally useless in getting her attention. With the menagerie of animals around, FatCat suffers to a significant degree from an inferiority complex. Her instincts are to chase the ducks and chickens, but they are all bigger, and chase her. So rather than be excluded for bad behaviour, she tries to join in, although she does draw the line at the duck pond.

Down by the riverside, in an old Victorian cottage and boathouse, lives Steve Smith, the cathedral Services Manager, with his wife Marcelle and their daughter Sian. This is another household where devotion to animals is apparent, but cats are clearly the heroes here. The house has been home to several pure-bred cats: Cleo and Nero, two Bengal cats, elegantly adorned the riverside gardens, until one day they were stolen. They were replaced by an Abyssinian female, from whom Sian hoped to breed. The neighbourhood tomcats helped out. So now the house has PJ, a mild-mannered and polite mostly-Abyssinian, who likes to sit at the foot of the steps leading up to the family's house. He's a real young gent, and completes the circle of cats that surround Worcester Cathedral. Sian is not too worried about PJ being taken from the public gardens, as he is watched over by a beady-eyed, stocky bull-terrier who is rather aptly named Fate.

OPPOSITE LEFT
A 'young gent' of a cat
BELOW
Markaduke waits for trombone practice to finish

Acknowledgements

St Edmundsbury Cathedral, Bury St Edmunds – Canon Andrew and the Rev. Catherine Todd

Canterbury Cathedral – Canon Richard and Mrs Elizabeth Marsh, Phoebe Marsh; Canon Edward and Mrs Sarah Condry

Chelmsford Cathedral – Mr Peter Nardone

Chester Cathedral – the Rt Rev. Dr Peter Forster, Bishop of Chester

Chichester Cathedral – the Rev. Nicholas and Mrs Marieke Biddle

Durham Cathedral – the Very Rev. Michael and Mrs Jennifer Sadgrove

St Mary's Episcopal Cathedral, Edinburgh – the Rev. William Mountsey, the Rev. Dean Fosterkew; Canon Jane Millard, Vice Provost

Ely Cathedral – Mr Martin and Mrs Paula Fleet; Mr Stephen and Mrs Stefanie Wikner; the Porter-Thaw family

Exeter Cathedral – Canon Neil Collings

Gloucester Cathedral – Canon David Hoyle

Hereford Cathedral – Mr Peter Dyke and Mr Shaun Ward. Hereford Cathedral photograph by D. Harbour, reproduced by kind permission of the Dean and Chapter of Hereford Cathedral

Lichfield Cathedral – Mr Mark Jervis

Portsmouth Cathedral – Mr David and Mrs Kitty Price

Ripon Cathedral – the Very Rev. John and Mrs Bridgit Methuen

Rochester Cathedral – Canon Jonathan and Mrs Rebecca Meyrick

Salisbury Cathedral – the Very Rev. June Osborne, Mr Steve Mellor

Southwell Minster – Canon Richard and Mrs Samantha Holgate Davey

Westminster Abbey – Canon David Hutt

Worcester Cathedral – Adrian and Joanna Lucas; Canon Alvyn and Mrs Judith Pettersen, Catherine Pettersen; Sian Smith